The Urbana Free Library

To renew: call **217-367-4057**
or go to **urbanafreelibrary.org**
and select **My Account**

spot

BABY FARM ANIMALS

LAMBS

by Anastasia Suen

AMICUS | AMICUS INK

lips

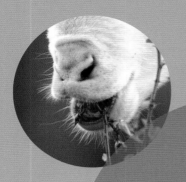

wool

Look for these words and pictures as you read.

legs

tail

Have you ever seen a lamb?
A lamb is a baby sheep.

Its mother is a ewe.
Some ewes have one lamb.
Some have two.

Look at the lamb's legs.
They are strong.
A lamb stands up the
day it is born.

legs

Look at the lamb's lips.
The top lip is split.
It can grab small leaves.

lips

tail

Look at the lamb's tail.
Some tails are short.
Some are long.

Look at the lamb's wool.
It grows thick and fluffy.
Wool is used to make clothes.

wool

A lamb lives with other sheep.
The flock is big.

Look at the lamb's lips.
The top lip is split.
It can grab small leaves.

lips

lips

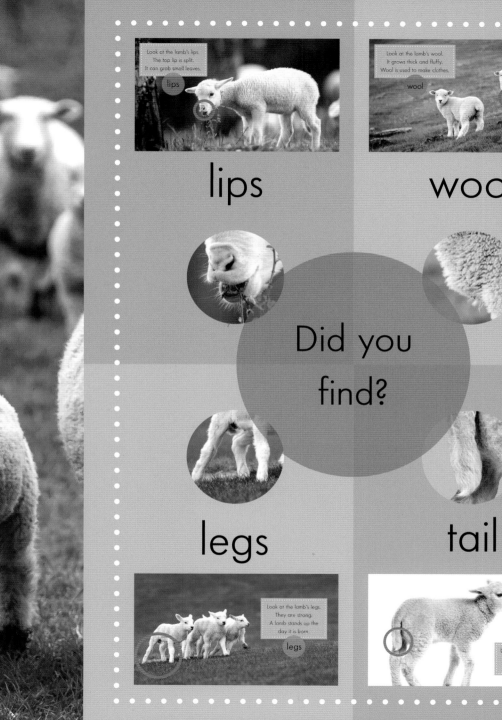

Look at the lamb's wool.
It grows thick and fluffy.
Wool is used to make clothes.

wool

wool

Did you find?

legs

tail

Look at the lamb's legs.
They are strong.
A lamb stands up the
day it is born.

legs

tail

Look at the lamb's tail.
Some tails are short.
Some are long.

spot

Spot is published by Amicus and Amicus Ink
P.O. Box 1329, Mankato, MN 56002
www.amicuspublishing.us

Library of Congress Cataloging-in-Publication Data
Names: Suen, Anastasia, author.
Title: Lambs / by Anastasia Suen.
Description: Mankato, MN : Amicus/Amicus Ink, [2019] | Series:
Spot. Baby farm animals | "Spot is published by Amicus." |
Audience: K to grade 3.
Identifiers: LCCN 2017053726 (print) | LCCN 2017054236
 (ebook) | ISBN 9781681515724 (pdf) | ISBN 9781681515342
 (library binding) | ISBN 9781681523729 (pbk.)
Subjects: LCSH: Lambs--Juvenile literature. | Farms--Juvenile
 literature. | Vocabulary.
Classification: LCC SF376.5 (ebook) | LCC SF376.5 .S84 2019
 (print) | DDC 636.3/07--dc23
LC record available at https://lccn.loc.gov/2017053726

Printed in China

HC 10 9 8 7 6 5 4 3 2 1
PB 10 9 8 7 6 5 4 3 2 1

Wendy Dieker and
  Mary Ellen Klukow, editors
Deb Miner, series designer
Aubrey Harper, book designer
Holly Young, photo researcher

Photos by Shutterstock/Eric Isselee
cover, 1, 10–11; iStock/GlobalP
cover, 4–5, 16, Filip_Krstic 2, 8–9,
15, WhitneyLewisPhotography 2,
12–13, 15, heebyj 14; Getty/Ernie
Hames/Nature Picture Library 2,
6–7, 15, georgeclerk 3

LAMBS